KAMA SUTRA

KAMA SUTRA

The Book of Sex Positions

SADIE CAYMAN

Racehorse Publishing

Disclaimer

Summersdale Publishers cannot be held responsible for any injuries or breakages that should occur when following the advice in this book. Always check on your partner's well-being when trying new positions – and please enjoy yourself carefully!

Contents

The sexual embrace can only be compared with music and with prayer.

Marcus Aurelius

Introduction

The Kama Sutra is an ancient Indian text, which has been reproduced and reimagined many times over the years and provides insights into having a happy, fulfilled life with your partner. The main reason it is known in the West is for its depictions of varied sexual positions, for a satisfying sex life. While this little book can't hope to reproduce all these teachings, we've hand-picked some of the best positions to let you know how they're done, which ones best suit your mood and how easy or tricky they are. In nearly all of these positions, frottage (rubbing together) can be substituted for penetration and still be enjoyed by both partners!

We hope this book will help you open your mind (and legs). Remember – make love, not war!

KISSING

Great sex isn't all about the act of penetration; the build-up is important, too! One of the best ways to build passion before the "main event" is sensual kissing, so this section gives you a small selection of the many ways in which the Kama Sutra suggests you enjoy your partner's lips.

The Bent Kiss

Passion:

Drama:

This is when each partner bends their head to the side and moves in for the kiss. It is often depicted with the passive partner leaning backwards, while the active partner leans over them, holding them close. A "classic" kiss, often seen at the romantic climax of films, this is popular among couples and can build great passion. It's also a great way to build heat before moving on to the main event!

The Turned Kiss

Passion:

Romance:

Like the bent kiss, this one is also a classic. The turned kiss is when the active partner takes the passive partner's chin in their hand, turning their partner's face towards them for a kiss. The active partner takes the lead, which adds a touch of passion to the moment. The passive partner may have turned away to be coy or playful, so this kiss is a way of saying "time for the next game".

The Kiss That Kindles Love

Effort:

Sexiness:

This one is a kiss for the partner who is usually passive. When your partner is sleeping and you feel that need for them building, use the kiss that kindles love as a slow, seductive way to wake them, ready for gentle lovemaking. Starting softly, this kiss can build into something more passionate as your partner awakens to the world, and to you.

Kiss me and you will see
how important I am.

Sylvia Plath

A kiss is a lovely trick designed by nature to stop speech when words become superfluous.

Ingrid Bergman

The Kiss That Turns Away

Compassion:

Happiness:

This kiss is to help your partner forget about their worries and bring their attention to you and your relationship. When they are worrying about work, distracted, or perhaps even when they are arguing with you, a gentle kiss that gradually becomes more intense will help move their attention away from the negative and back to the happiness of your embrace.

The Demonstrative Kiss

Suggestiveness:

Devotion:

This kiss is one to show your desire for your partner, either in public or in private. Indeed, this sort of kiss doesn't even have to include both partners directly. These kisses are a visual way to say, "I want you" – sometimes within a crowded room. One partner could, for example, kiss their finger while looking the other in the eyes. When alone, kissing your partner softly on the back of their leg is a good example of the demonstrative kiss.

ORAL
PLEASURE

Oral sex is, for many, a key part of sexual union. It can either be part of the build-up or can form the main event. The ancient Kama Sutra did not put much stock in oral sex, viewing it as the work of eunuchs or concubines, but the world has moved on since then and many re-imaginings of the Kama Sutra have moved their focus to the intimate pleasure oral sex can provide. In this section, we describe some of the best positions for pleasuring each other orally.

Solo Fellatio

Eroticism:

Intimacy:

After feasting your eyes on your partner's body, let your mouth get in on the action with this simple act of oral stimulation – it's the best job you'll ever have.

If your partner is male, there might be times when you just want to pleasure them and enjoy the process. According to the *Kama Sutra*, the act of fellatio should be performed in several stages, gradually progressing: it should start with a gentle touch of the lips, moving on to kissing, stroking and pressing your body against your partner's intimate zone, before graduating to full oral penetration. A gentle approach should be used, building up to be more intense if you and your partner wish it to.

Solo Cunnilingus

Eroticism:

Intimacy:

Nibbling on ear lobes is all well and good, but head south to your lady's primary pleasure zone to pay some real lip service. Go on – *yoni* you want to!

Just as with solo fellatio, if your partner is female there might be times when you just want to give them pleasure and enjoy doing it. According to the Kama Sutra, the way of kissing a woman's yoni (vagina) should already be known, through having kissed the mouth. This is a good place to start from, but certainly not the whole story! As with fellatio, begin gently with kisses and caresses. Use your mouth to explore the whole of her intimate area, not just the clitoris. Some women enjoy penetration with the tongue, too. Try different levels of pressure with your tongue and lips to find out what your partner enjoys.

Doggy Style

Stimulation: ▼ ▼ ▼ ▼ ▽

Romance: ▼ ▼ ▽ ▽ ▽

Unleash your inner animal with this all-fours oral buffet.

Although more commonly known as a penetrative sex position, the doggy style position can be put to great use for oral sex. One partner goes onto all fours and the other can kneel behind them to give pleasure that way (either vaginally or anally for a female partner; anally for a male). If that's not what you fancy, then the giving partner can lie with their head below the receiving partner's intimate region and tease and please them from below.

Classic "69"

Two-way pleasure:

🩲 🩲 🩲 🩲 🩲

Danger of accidental kneeing-in-the-face:

🩲 🩲 🩲 🩲 🩲

They say two heads are better than one – and that goes for the bedroom, too. Deliver and receive pleasure simultaneously with this top-to-tail classic.

Once you've mastered the solo basics, the natural progression is to enjoy oral sex together. The most commonly known way to do this is the classic "69", named for the shape the two lovers make when they are in this position. In the *Kama Sutra*, this is referred to as "congress of a crow".

For a 69, one partner lies on their back with the other on top – "top-to-tail" – so the bottom partner's head is in line with their partner's intimate region and vice versa. Then it's just a question of using the skills you've practised in solo oral sex. For many, the 69 and its related positions are a great way to have full-body intimacy with a partner and can lead to simultaneous orgasm.

Side
"69"

Exertion: ▼ ▼ ▼ ▽ ▽

Convenience: ▼ ▼ ▼ ▼ ▼

Life is hard enough without making sexy-time a chore. With this super-comfortable position, you can get all the oral pleasure with none of the effort.

Like the classic, this is a simple "69" position, but rather than being one on top of the other, each partner can lie on their side in a comfortable position, with their face nuzzled between their partner's legs. This is perfect for laid-back, lazy sex, when you want maximum enjoyment with minimum exertion.

Sex appeal is the keynote of our civilisation.

Henri Bergson

I write about sex because often it feels like the most important thing in the world.

Jeanette Winterson

The Lap of Luxury

Difficulty:

Pleasure:

Sit back, relax and lap it up from the comfort of the couch with this orgasmic option.

This is pure laziness for the partner receiving oral pleasure. Using your favorite chair, or the sofa, the passive partner sits back comfortably while the active partner kneels in front and pleasures them. The passive partner can use their hands to guide the giver, talking to them and telling them what they want, or they can just sit back, relax and enjoy the ride.

The Face Sit

Playfulness:

Tantalisation:

Oral on your mind? It will be hard to think of anything else if you embrace the face with this tantalising teaser.

In this position, the receiver becomes the active partner. The giver lies on the bed (or floor, sofa, etc.) with their head supported by pillows. The receiving partner then kneels over the giver's face and gently lowers their body until the giver can provide oral pleasure. The giver can support the receiver by holding their hips or bottom, while the receiver can lean their hands on the wall or bedframe for extra support if needed. This position is ideal for teasing, particularly if the giver really enjoys the part they play – the receiver can move just out of reach, leaving the giver wanting and heightening the sense of play.

LAID BACK

Roll out the shag rug, fill up the water bed and plump up the velvet pillows; it's time to lie back and get laid. These classic positions allow for at least one partner to chill out and ride the high. And don't worry – if you can't decide whose turn it is to be on top, then there are a few positions where both lazy lovers can enjoy themselves.

Bandoleer

Flexibility:

Pleasure:

Lock and load, people, it's time to go deep. Find your feet with this lustful, languid position that allows fathomless penetration with all the comfort you could desire. It is ideal for lingering, lazy fun.

Start with the passive partner on their back, with their head supported by a comfy cushion. The active partner should kneel in front of them, close enough for the lucky passive person to rest their feet on their partner's chest. The passive partner can rest their thighs and bottom on the active's thighs; if this is not comfortable, they can support the small of their back with fluffy pillows. The active partner can then slowly enter, gradually building to deeper, harder penetration. If the passive partner is feeling dextrous, they can give additional pleasure with manual stimulation.

The Glowing Triangle

Exertion:

Closeness:

You'll both be glowing after this hot and heavy hip-thruster, where for a change the partner on the bottom works their ass off, so to speak.

The glowing triangle is roughly based on the missionary position, where the passive partner lies on their back and the active partner climbs on top and does all the "work". In this version, however, things are a little different.

The active partner lies on their back, ready for penetration, with their hips tilted upwards. Their hips can be supported by a pillow if this is more comfortable. The passive partner then gets onto all fours and enters their partner, who then, holding on to the passive partner's back or shoulders for support, uses the action of their hips, back and forth, to achieve deeper penetration – doing all the "work"!

Nirvana

Sensuality:

Stimulation:

Reinforce the bedposts and warn the neighbours as you thrust off to coital cloud nine.

This position works best with a female passive partner, as it provides extra clitoral stimulation which can make orgasm faster and more intense.

The passive partner lies on their back with their hands raised above their head, holding on to the headboard or bedposts. They keep their legs closed as far as possible. The active partner then climbs on top, their legs spread, and penetrates their partner. The passive partner's pressed-together thighs heighten the penetrative sensation, as well as providing additional clitoral stimulation.

Sex lies at the
root of life, and we can
never learn to reverence
life until we know how
to understand sex.

Havelock Ellis

Each of us is born with
a box of matches inside
us but we can't strike
them all by ourselves.

Laura Esquivel

Supernova

Exertion:

Intensity:

Ready for some stratospheric sexual congress? Reach for the stars with this explosive experience.

Start with the passive partner lying on the bed (make sure their head is either near to the foot of the bed or they're lying perpendicular to the pillows). The active partner then straddles them in a typical "cowgirl" position for penetration, rocking back and forth until climax is imminent. The active partner then stops moving, puts weight through their knees and, holding their partner's torso, moves them towards the edge of the bed so their head, shoulders and arms hang down to the floor: the active partner begins moving again until climax is reached. The blood rushing to the passive partner's head will enhance the sensitivity of their upper body and the intensity of their orgasm.

The Clip

Sexiness: ▼ ▼ ▼ ▼ ▽

Stimulation: ▼ ▼ ▼ ▼ ▼

Feel the rhythm, feel the ride... Try this slip and slide supine stance for great penetration, manual stimulation and a full-frontal view.

In this relatively simple position, it is the partner being penetrated who is most active.

The passive partner lies on their back, legs closed. The active partner then straddles them, allowing for penetration, and leans back using their hands for support. Once in position, the active partner uses a sliding movement to build rhythm, while the passive partner can reach out to stroke their skin or give them additional pleasure using their hand.

The Splitting Bamboo

Flexibility:

Satisfaction:

Bamboo might not make pandas frisky, but you're sure to be a herbaceous convert after this leg-bending little number.

Don't let the word "splitting" put you off this one! It is an easy-to-do position and great for slow, lazy lovemaking.

To split the bamboo, the passive partner lies on their back with one leg slightly bent. The active partner straddles this leg, then the passive partner lifts their other leg and drapes it over the active partner's shoulder, so that their legs form a scissor-like shape. While a gradual, sliding rhythm is built, the passive partner can reach down and help things along with a little manual stimulation.

The Curled Angel

Flexibility: ▼ ▽ ▽ ▽ ▽

Comfort: ▼ ▼ ▼ ▼ ▽

Forks at the ready, it's time to spoon in style with a spot of cosy, curled coitus.

If you've ever heard the phrase "spooning leads to forking", this position is proof.

The person who will be penetrated curls up and their partner curls behind them, spooning them. Penetration from this angle is soft and easy – perfect for a laid-back Sunday morning. This position also allows the active partner to reach round to please the passive partner with their hand.

The curled angel is often favoured by pregnant women as it is gentler and avoids squashing the baby bump.

The Tigress

Exertion:

Stimulation:

This one really should be called "the lion" because you'll be roaring like one in no time.

This position is more commonly known as "reverse cowgirl". In a similar way to "the clip", the partner who is penetrated is doing the bulk of the work, so the passive partner can enjoy the view. The passive partner lies down with their legs together, while the active partner straddles them with their back to their partner, facing their feet. Once penetrated, the active partner then rocks up and down, arching their back. They may want to place a hand back on their partner's chest for support. The passive partner can then caress them from behind or hold them round the waist from behind to control the rhythm.

THE
LOVE SEAT

A natural progression from the "easier" supine positions, seated positions can give you the chance to have greater contact with your partner, deeper penetration and a new way of experiencing each other.

The Rocking Horse

Intimacy:

Suppleness:

The best pony ride in town – saddle up for this climactic canter and you'll both be hurtling over the finish line in no time.

In this position, the person being penetrated becomes the active partner. The passive partner sits cross-legged, perhaps supported by cushions. They can also use their hands for extra support. The active partner then kneels over the passive partner's lap, lowering their body down until penetration is achieved. They can hold their partner for support as they use a bouncing or swaying motion to build speed and penetration.

This is a great position for romance, as you can gaze into your partner's eyes throughout.

Crouching Tiger

Difficulty: ▼ ▼ ▼ ▽ ▽

Agility: ▼ ▼ ▼ ▼ ▽

This wildcat workout doesn't require any special martial arts moves, but it will leave you and your partner purring with pleasure.

This position takes its name from the crouching position of the passive partner. The active partner lies on their back at the edge of the bed, with their feet on the floor. The passive partner then squats over the active partner to achieve penetration. Both the movements of the active and passive partners can build momentum in this position, depending on who wants more control. The active partner can hold their partner's bottom if they want more control over movement. During this position, the passive partner's hands are free to give extra pleasure to their partner, or themselves.

The Frog

Sensuality: 🩲🩲🩲🩲🩲

Balance: 🩲🩲🩲🩲🩲

Need a bit more bounce in your bedroom? Try this amphibian-inspired position for a flirty fumble in the jungle.

This position is somewhat similar to the crouching tiger, in that the passive partner squats over the active one. In the frog, however, both partners are sitting rather than lying down. This enables a greater sense of closeness and intimacy, letting the passive partner feel held and secure.

The active partner sits at the edge of the bed, leaving room for the passive partner to squat over them. The passive partner lowers their body, back to their partner, using their hands to balance like a frog. Once in position, either the passive partner's bouncing movement or the active partner's thrusting can control the rhythm.

Catherine Wheel

Flexibility:

Stimulation:

Get ready for a feel-good fireworks explosion, with intertwined limbs and perfect penetration. Oooh! Aaah!

In the Catherine wheel, both partners are seated. Begin by facing each other, lean back, and shift your bodies towards each other until penetration is possible. Each partner then wraps their legs around the other, entwining themselves and leaning back, resting their hands on the bed or floor for extra support. A gentle rubbing or grinding motion can be used to start with, gradually building energy to climax.

The moment eternal –
just that and no more.

When ecstasy's utmost
we clutch at the core.

Robert Browning

Variety, multiplicity are the two most powerful vehicles of lust.

Marquis de Sade

Kneeling Congress

Stamina:

Closeness:

Bring each other to your knees for some serious bumping and grinding with this mutual meeting of body parts.

Otherwise known as "the kneel", this is a great position for intimacy. Not only do you face each other, so can look directly into your partner's eyes, you get full body contact as well as heightened sensitivity as different parts of your bodies brush and press together.

To achieve kneeling bliss, the active partner keeps their legs together, while the passive partner straddles them, allowing for penetration. The passive partner can then wrap their arms around the active partner's neck and move in for a kiss, while the active partner develops a slow, gentle rhythm.

Milk and Water Embrace

Stimulation:

Intimacy:

Are you sitting comfortably? You will be once you take a seat and settle into this steamy session.

Don't worry, there's no milk or water required, but to get started you'll need an armless chair – the edge of the bed could work, too. The penetrating partner takes a seat and the other person sits on their lap facing away from them, letting their partner's hands wander all over their body. When you're both aroused and ready for more, the partner on top repositions their body for penetration, still seated and facing away from their partner. The top partner rocks back and forth, while the other person continues to pleasure them with their hands.

The Spider

Exertion:

Core strength:

This sexy face-to-face frisson will leave you both tangled in a web of sweat and sheets.

Sit on the bed facing each other. The penetrating partner sits with their legs stretched out in front of them, supporting themselves with their arms behind them; their partner, who is actually more active in this position, sits on their lap with their legs bent either side of the penetrating partner's chest. The shape you'll make together is like one giant erotic spider! The active partner leans all their body weight back onto their hands – this way they can rock their hips easily and effectively, bringing both of you to climax.

TAKE A STAND

Here we look at some of the standing positions which have been inspired by the Kama Sutra. They're perhaps more adventurous – especially as they tend to be more energetic and can easily be done outside the bedroom – and though some are supported, they can require quite a lot of strength and stamina!

The Padlock

Comfort: ▼ ▼ ▽ ▽ ▽

Raunchiness: ▼ ▼ ▼ ▼ ▼

Forget balls and chains (well, maybe not balls), and get locked up together with this table-testing love-in.

In this position, the active partner is standing while the passive partner sits on top of a high piece of furniture, such as a table or kitchen counter, and uses their arms for support. The active partner stands in front and the passive partner wraps their legs around them, pulling them in close for deep penetration. The active partner could lean on the surface for balance, or take hold of their partner's bottom to control the speed and depth of penetration.

The Ascent to Desire

Ease:

Workout level:

Elevate your relationship to new heights while testing your strength and stamina. This mountainous manoeuvre might take a while to master, but the view from the top will be worth it.

This could be seen as the "classic" standing position; it requires at least one partner to be strong, with plenty of stamina.

The active partner stands with their knees slightly bent, making sure they are firmly balanced, then lifts the passive partner up. The passive partner wraps their legs around the active partner's hips for penetration and their arms around their partner's shoulders for closeness and stability. If it helps, the passive partner can balance their feet on the edge of the bed or back of the sofa to take some of their own weight. The downward action of the passive partner's weight makes this a position for very deep penetration, as well as providing a damn good workout!

The body is an instrument which only gives off music when it is used as a body.

Anais Nin

To have her here in bed
with me, breathing
on me... I count that
something of a miracle.

Henry Miller

The Plough

Flexibility:

Carnality:

This upright twist on doggy style takes farm-assured friskiness to a new level. It's like gardening, but sexier.

Though not strictly a completely upright position, this does require the active partner to stand and to have plenty of stamina.

To achieve the plough position the passive partner lies on their front at the end of the bed, legs over the edge. The active partner then lifts the passive partner's legs and holds them, either side of their hips, while moving in for penetration. The passive partner uses their elbows for support while the active partner holds them up and controls things from behind – the active partner is fully in control in this position.

The Lustful Leg

Strength:

Flexibility:

Limber up, lovers, and let your legs do all the work. This bendy, sexy pose is ideal for flexible bodies.

This is a little more adventurous than the padlock or the ascent to desire, and requires more strength, flexibility and balance, but the result can be great – especially if you enjoy deeper penetration.

Start by facing each other. The passive partner should rest one leg on the bed, or another surface, then the active partner bends down and lifts the leg onto their shoulder. The passive partner wraps their arms around their partner's neck, allowing their body to be pulled in for penetration. The active partner holds on to their partner's bottom for extra support and to control their thrusts.

The Challenge

Agility: ▼▼▼▼▽

Intimacy: ▼▼▼▽▽

Feel the burn and the yearn when you work those thigh muscles and your partner in this impressive feat of sexual vigour.

This aptly-named position is trickier than your average standing stance and requires plenty of leg strength and balance from the passive partner. You'll also need a good, sturdy chair, or something similar.

The passive partner stands on the chair and bends into a sitting position, elbows on knees with their legs taking their weight. The active partner then enters from behind, keeping hold of their partner's waist or bottom for added balance and control.

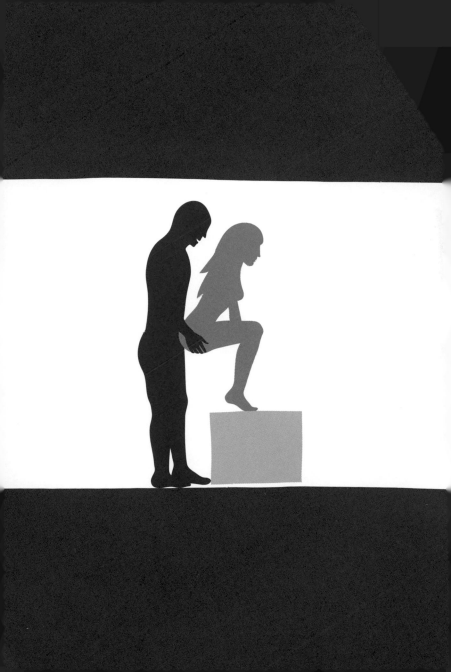

The Column

Sexiness:

Comfort:

Columns are tall and hard, right? Sounds like a good recipe for some orgasmic action.

For this one, both partners stand in a spooning position with the active partner behind the passive one. Snuggle closely, so your arms are intertwined for intimacy and leverage. The active partner penetrates from behind – if the active partner is considerably taller, they'll have to squat down; if they are smaller they could stand on a step or a small stool. While the active partner controls the thrusting from behind, the passive partner arches their back and leans slightly forward. Try leaning against a wall or over a chair to allow for deeper penetration.

Crossed Keys

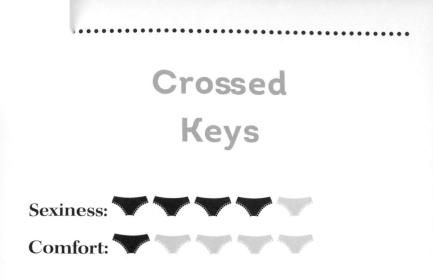

Sexiness:

Comfort:

Crossing your fingers that this next position will give you the thrills and chills your body craves? Why not try crossing your legs instead...

This position requires just the active partner to stand, but it's simple, effective and can be adapted to suit the flexibility of the passive partner. The passive partner lies on a hip-height table or a high bed with their bottom positioned on the edge. They should point their feet towards the ceiling, crossing their legs at the knees. The active partner penetrates from a standing position, holding their partner's legs and crossing and uncrossing them as they do so. The squeezing will contribute to the passive partner's orgasm.

FAR-OUT POSITIONS

If you think you've tried it all and got the T-shirt, why not attempt some of the more adventurous suggestions in this section? These are not for the faint of heart: they will not only challenge your stamina, but in some cases your balance, too!

The Propeller

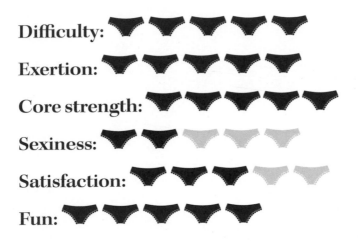

Difficulty: 🩲🩲🩲🩲🩲

Exertion: 🩲🩲🩲🩲🩲

Core strength: 🩲🩲🩲🩲🩲

Sexiness: 🩲🩲🩲🩲🩲

Satisfaction: 🩲🩲🩲🩲🩲

Fun: 🩲🩲🩲🩲🩲

Prepare to take your relationship to new heights with this deceptively complicated coupling.

The passive partner lies on their back with their legs stretched out and their thighs positioned slightly apart. The active partner lies on top of them, straddling their waist, but facing away from them with their feet towards their partner's head. This angle is difficult for penetration, so it might be easier for the active partner to penetrate when kneeling and then lie down afterwards. As the active lover thrusts they rotate a full 360 degrees, staying inside of their reclining lover. The eroticism is heightened by the fact that your partner is facing away from you and you can both focus solely on the sensation.

Love is composed of a single soul inhabiting two bodies.

Aristotle

Sex is as important as eating or drinking, and we ought to allow the one appetite to be satisfied with as little restraint or false modesty as the other.

Marquis de Sade

The Erotic V

Core strength: ♥ ♥ ♥ ♥ ♡

Satisfaction: ♥ ♥ ♥ ♥ ♥

With a bit of practice and a good warm-up stretch, this great V position will deliver the big O and more.

This is a challenging seated/standing position, which requires stability. The passive partner rests their bottom at the edge of a table or other firm surface. The active partner stands in front of them and lets their partner rest a leg against each of their shoulders. The passive partner can wrap their arms around the active partner's neck for extra support. The active partner enters, achieving very deep penetration.

The Ape

Lasciviousness: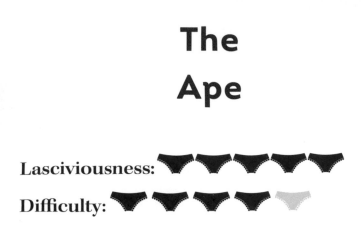

Difficulty:

No more monkeying around – it's time to get serious. This position isn't for amateurs, but if you do it right you'll be crowned king of the swingers in no time.

This is an "advanced" position and requires strength, stamina, flexibility and balance. For all that it requires, though, it can give intense pleasure as it enables deep, controlled penetration.

The passive partner lies on their back and pulls their knees up to their chest. A more supportive firm surface, such as the floor, is better for this position. The active partner then sits back to allow penetration, resting their back on the passive partner's feet, and controls penetration by moving up and down. They can reach back and hold their partner's wrists for extra support if needed.

The Rowing Boat

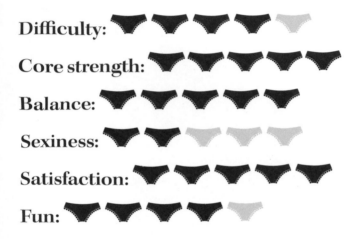

Difficulty: ▼▼▼▼▽

Core strength: ▼▼▼▼▼

Balance: ▼▼▼▼▼

Sexiness: ▼▼▽▽▽

Satisfaction: ▼▼▼▼▼

Fun: ▼▼▼▼▽

This seated position may look simple, but to row to victory you're going to need an oar-ful lot of determination.

The active partner lies down, while the passive partner straddles them for penetration. Once in position, the active partner then rises to a seated position, with their knees bent and lifted – supported by their partner's arms. The passive partner repositions their body slightly to mirror their partner.

The active partner places their hands underneath their partner bottom to help control penetration. The position is tricky to master, but the face-to-face intimacy more than makes up for the hard work.

Sex is always about emotions. Good sex is about free emotions; bad sex is about blocked emotions.

Deepak Chopra

Sex appeal is
50 per cent what you've
got and 50 per cent what
people think you've got.

Sophia Loren

The Bridge

Sensuality: ▼ ▼ ▼ ▼ ▽

Exertion: ▼ ▼ ▼ ▼ ▼

Time to whip out those yoga moves, sans stretchy leggings, and bridge that gap between average and mind-blowing sex.

First, the partner who will be penetrating forms the bridge by bending over backwards. Then the passive partner straddles them, lowering themselves down gently to achieve penetration. It is then the passive partner who becomes active, using the motion of their legs to control penetration.

It is advised that you don't stay in this position for too long – you wouldn't want to collapse with all that blood rushing to your head! This one really is for the super strong and flexible only. Good luck!

The Suspended Scissors

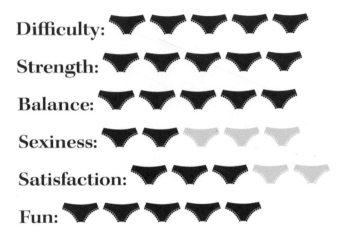

Difficulty:

Strength:

Balance:

Sexiness:

Satisfaction:

Fun:

If you want to try something truly athletic, this may be for you. It might look like a naughty game of Twister, but this dose of scissor-legged sensuality is for grown-ups only.

The passive partner rests their calves and feet on the edge of the bed, with one arm holding their body up from the floor, while the active partner supports them at the waist.

The active partner then straddles their partner's lower leg, helping to hold the upper leg, and penetrates the passive partner while they balance.

This may sound complex but if you have the strength and stamina needed, the natural stimulation from the scissor position, along with the rush of blood to the passive partner's head, can lead to amazing orgasms.

It is not sex that gives the pleasure, but the lover.

Marge Piercy

There is a
charm about the
forbidden that makes it
unspeakably desirable.

Mark Twain

Conclusion

We hope you've enjoyed this book and that it's given you some food for thought! Whichever way you choose to use it – as a mini-guide or reference book, or just to get your own ideas flowing – we hope that it will help enhance your sex life and bring you and your partner closer together. Perhaps you will go on to read the original Kama Sutra and appreciate the wide knowledge of happy relationships it has continued to impart for centuries!

Checklist

- ☐ The bent kiss

- ☐ The turned kiss

- ☐ The kiss that kindles love

- ☐ The kiss that turns away

- ☐ The demonstrative kiss

- ☐ Solo fellatio

- ☐ Solo cunnilingus

- ☐ Doggy style

- ☐ Classic "69"

- ☐ Side "69"

- ☐ The lap of luxury

- ☐ The face sit

- ☐ **Bandoleer**

- ☐ **The glowing triangle**

- ☐ **Nirvana**

- ☐ **Supernova**

- ☐ **The clip**

- ☐ **The splitting bamboo**

- ☐ **The curled angel**

- ☐ **The tigress**

- ☐ **The rocking horse**

- ☐ **Crouching tiger**

- ☐ **The frog**

- ☐ **Catherine wheel**

- [ ] **Kneeling congress**

- [ ] **Milk and water embrace**

- [ ] **The spider**

- [ ] **The padlock**

- [ ] **The ascent to desire**

- [ ] **The plough**

- [ ] **The lustful leg**

- [ ] **The challenge**

- [ ] **The column**

- [ ] **Crossed keys**

- [ ] **The propeller**

- [ ] **The erotic õ**

- [ ] **The ape**

••

☐   The rowing boat

☐   The bridge

☐   The suspended scissors

••

If you're interested in finding out more about our books, find us on Facebook at **Skyhorse Publishing** and follow us on Twitter and Instagram at **@skyhorsepub**.

www.skyhorsepublishing.com